Things We Don't Tell

Things We Don't Tell

A Memoir in Poetry

Beautiful V. Lawson

Published by Meet the World Image Solutions
www.mtwimagesolutions.com

Cover design by Meet the World Image Solutions

ISBN: 979-8-9872429-9-5

*To my soulmate, here is
my official introduction to you.*

Contents

Acknowledgments ix

Introduction 1

Heartbreak 2

Pariah 5

Me 10

A Pedophile 12

Art 14

Softie 16

You 20

Dear Black Men 23

Fairy Tales 28

4 + 9 31

Lakee 34

About the Author 36

Acknowledgments

I'd like to thank my family for supporting my
journey on finding myself again.
I'd like to thank Queen Sheba, Grammy Award
winner and Master Poet, for instructing me in
channeling my thoughts into art.
Thank you, Mom, for laying the foundation and
allowing me the platform to be myself. I love you.

Introduction

This book is for men and women who have ever wanted to be in love, have been in love, or have gotten their hearts broken. In my poems, I take you on a journey through my memories of past relationships with men and women.

I also let you into my inner thoughts; the things I either didn't have the confidence to say out loud or didn't have the words to articulate into a proper conversation. From reading my poetry, I hope you're able to reflect on your own relationship experiences. I believe the best way to deter yourself from making the same mistakes in new relationships is to sit with yourself and evaluate what went wrong. What differences could you have made that would have changed the trajectory of your future?

I'll be asking a series of those questions to help you with that process.

Heartbreak

When opportunity arose,
I chose to dance with the idea of being the villain.
I created endless scenarios
Of burning the world to the ground,
Endless scenarios of tearing everything apart.
I danced with the Devil.
In my mind, I was Queen Dagmar,
As if everything I've done in my life has been
prepping me for this moment,
And as the queen of Hell, I was determined to not
stop until the world fell.
However, my two left feet
And both sides of my brain
And the will I have left
Forced me to stop standing on his feet.

Heart Notes

How did it feel the last time you were rejected? Some people may have a fear of going into this depressive state. I'd be lying if I said that wasn't me at a certain point. However, I wrote this during a time of choosing not to be the victim anymore.

I wrote Heartbreak after thinking of all the different scenarios of being the cruelest person on earth because I let someone hurt my feelings. I thought of what life would be like if I just chose to stop being the bigger person and stopped considering anyone else. Sometimes, hurt people build a thick wall, and they leave it up for so long, they would have to fight tooth and nail to tear it back down.

I imagined a part of myself locked into a concrete box, trying to heal from having my feelings hurt, while the villain in me took over for damage control. If you decided to become the villain, would you be happier?

In my mind, I imagined what it would have been like to dance with the Devil. My reality reminded me that I can't dance, and I can't allow myself to let evil guide me.

Pariah

I'm emotionally unavailable, and I don't know
how to fix it.
I want it so badly,
But I'm so tired of the work that I've put into it.
So now I'm emotionally unavailable,
And I don't know how to fix it.
I ponder.
I wonder.
Is this another tribulation?
Am I meant to be unavailable?
Is it supposed to be fixed?
Am I meant to be unavailable?
Is there something I don't get?
Have I met the problem?
Or am I in the process of fixing it?
Am I someone who needs to be fixed?
Or maybe I'm unavailable because I haven't met
the person

Who was meant to consider me in every situation.
Maybe the problem isn't me,
But the people who surround me.
Maybe even now, as I try to recognize what the
pattern is
I haven't realized that the pattern is
I'm always considering myself in situations
Where others should be considering me.
That's why I'm emotionally unavailable,
And I can't seem to fix it.
Because, as of right now,
That part of me will stay asleep.
The consideration in me will stay asleep.
Because she is so tired of all of the work
She's been putting into me.
She is unfazed
By the hurtful names
People may use to wake her up.
She is unfazed
By those names
Because only another consideration
Will wake her up.

A reminder that she does not have to work,
A reminder that she does not have to cry,
A reminder that she does not have to be angry,
A reminder that she is not alone
Are the only names that will wake her up.
I'm emotionally unavailable
And I don't need to fix it.

Heart Notes

What does the beginning of a healthy relationship look like to you?

I think it looks like being absorbed in my hobbies and letting my partner take notice of what I'm passionate about. It doesn't look like I actively sought them out or constantly plastered a smile on my face. My partner has gotten to see me in my most natural light before considering a commitment to me.

God puts us through things so we can learn from them, and I like to think I haven't found the right person yet because they are dealing with something I haven't learned how to help them with yet. If there's nothing left to learn from the contenders I've already met, that would mean this is the time for me to pour into myself. I'm choosing to focus more on figuring out what I'm good at and what could be better, so when that partner does come around,

I'll have something to show for all the time we were apart.

Me

I want children one day,
And when I look at my babies,
I want to be reminded of
The love I have for you,
Not the regret I have for myself.

Heart Notes

What do you look for in a partner, and what do you want out of them long term? When people ask me, "Do you have children?" My favorite answer to give them is "No, I haven't found someone who deserves my children."

I would want my partner to have the same mentality. I like to think God gave us the ability to make children because they're supposed to embody the overflowing love you have for each other. My fear is to be with someone who wants to have kids with just anyone. Not only would it be traumatic to me and our relationship, but now I've invited my first child into a world with no guide on how to navigate people. How can I expect my first son or daughter to respect themselves and make sound decisions when this is the example I've set for them?

A Pedophile

You made us laugh,
You made us cry,
And you were proud of your lies.
Two baby girls were your prize
For victimizing young girls' lives.
A baby girl went to school.
Who knew the world would be so cruel?
For you to find and send your crew
To give her dreams that were untrue.
Like a thief in the night.
Another girl to feed your pride.
Sent her away from family
For a child she would have, but couldn't be.

Heart Notes

How did you survive your childhood? Sometimes I wish I could go back to a world where I thought everyone was good, and adults only wanted the best for children. Now, as an adult hearing about all the crooked people in movies, our music, and our politics, I realize why children are made to be so blind.

No child should ever have to experience being a victim. I wrote this poem when I thought about the types of rewards and repercussions these kinds of people get. Fame, money, children ... these things build their lives in silence. The more I learn, the more I understand how carefully the systems are designed to protect power, not innocence. And sometimes, it makes me wonder if healing is even possible in a world that keeps celebrating those who do the most harm.

But writing helps me name the darkness, even if I can't erase it.

Art

Can you make art out of simplicity?
Loving you is like shining a light in a blind
woman's face.
You never hid who you were,
But I was so determined to love you
And be with you,
That I couldn't see the evil you projected onto me.
I mistook your flashing lights for sunlight.
I confused your bright days and your dark nights.
And when I think about you,
I regret what I remember.

Heart Notes

How did you feel after you ended your worst relationship? Have you ever stopped talking about an ex because of the em-barrassment that went along with it?

Even saying their name feels like admitting you let someone like that into your life, into your heart. It's hard to explain how you could love someone who broke you in such invisible ways, but sometimes love isn't about what we see, but what we're hoping to feel. And I hoped so hard that I ignored the harm.

This poem is me forgiving the version of myself that didn't know better. The version that called chaos "passion" and silence "peace." I'm not writing this for closure, but for clarity. Because pretending it didn't happen only buries the truth deeper.

Softie

You wouldn't know hard if it broke your walls,
And your army of guards had been taken down.
You wouldn't know it if it were a hit to the heart
And your smile turned into a frown.
And never for a moment at night
Does that frown go away
As you lie awake wondering what
He's been doing all day.
You try to ask, but his answers are vague,
And that ends the conversation,
So, in silence, you'll stay.
Hard is realizing the first person
You loved is a pervert.
Hard is knowing the second person you loved
hates gays and therefore hates you.
Hard is knowing the third person you loved
doesn't know if he loves you,
And he won't commit to you,

But says he'll be there for you as he fucks you
over and over again,
And you just don't know what to do.
Hard is wanting to seek help and not wanting to
protect him.
Hard is believing he's good
With good intentions and good for you.
Hard is believing you'll never say I do
Because it seems that man you're looking for isn't
looking for you.
Hard is knowing deep down he found "her,"
thinking she was you,
Or he knew her all along and they were just
playing a big-ass mind game with you
Hard is knowing that he loves her, too.

Heart Notes

What was the last conversation you had with yourself? I wrote Softie when I realized how fragile I could be. There are only so many times I could brush things off my shoulders and say they don't bother me. I found myself slowly making myself go insane trying to convince myself that I had a personality trait I never had.

For some reason, I wouldn't admit I had the ability to become paranoid, jealous, or sad. Why? Are these not human traits? I pushed those things so far into my mental abyss that I fell into a deep depression. I never handled my feelings in the moments that mattered and almost let them take over me. I thought being strong meant being unaffected, that silence equaled strength, and indifference was power. But all that did was make me a stranger to myself.

I ignored warning signs like sleepless nights and the way I flinched at kindness like it was a trick. I wore detachment like armor, not realizing it was keeping me from healing. Writing Softie was the first time I gave those buried emotions a voice. It reminded me that softness isn't weakness. It's honesty. It's survival.

You

You're the missing piece to my puzzle.
The culprit of my stress,
Yet the key to my prayers.
I've been having a sense of imbalance
Due to your absence,
Yet, you continue your distance.
I've begged for your presence,
Prayed for your existence,
Pondered on why you haven't come home to me,
Yet you continue your distance.
I wonder.
I wonder if the reason for your absence,
The reason for your nonexistence,
The clue as to why you stay away
Is because, as I continue on myself
And build from my failures,
I haven't yet reached the final point—
The boss level of life.

For you to be my prize for not taking myself away.
I live for you and the life we could have.
I build for you.
That's why I will stay.

Heart Notes

If your soulmate were standing in front of you right now, what would you say to them? I like to believe I haven't met mine yet because there's something I need to learn from life first. Maybe I need to recognize the parts of me that still crave healing, patience, and purpose.

I think my heart still needs to grow in ways only solitude and time can teach. I don't want to meet this person before I'm ready, before I can fully see *them*, and not just the idea of them.

I want to meet them when I'm whole enough to love without fear, and wise enough to be loved the same way.

Dear Black Men

Hey there, big boy,
Look what you're doing.
Hey there, big boy,
Look what you're doing.
Dear Black men,
Thank you for your appreciation,
But the whole female nation didn't ask for your
approval.
I'll give you my smile when I get my break.
Calling at me from across the street isn't sexy;
It makes my stomach ache.
Keep your comments until they're invited.
Always the same damn thing,
With the same damn words,
Like you're a part of Black Men United.
Don't get my targeting twisted.
All assholes are the same,
Except they come in different shades.

When we were young,

They told us confidence is key.

Dear all men,

Your overconfidence disgusts me.

Hey there, big boy

Look what you're doing.

Hey there, big boy,

Look what you're doing.

"Tryna smash these hoes,"

Be a rapist for your bros,

Smashed the wrong hoe,

Cut it off, second hole.

Apologies.

A bit too graphic.

"I'm not really like that,"

"I'm just acting,"

Is what he used to tell me.

Your second personality.

But who's the one I'm dating?

Hey there, big boy,

Look what you're doing.

Hey there, big boy,

Look what you're doing.
You're probably sitting there thinking,
"What about you?"
"I know you ain't through cause you hoes do it,
too."
"But not as much as you,"
These hoes say in reply.
An endless argument on both sides.

Heart Notes

How do you express yourself? This was my first poem, written in my first poetry class in my undergrad at Clark Atlanta University. Queen Sheba had given us a variety of poetry exercises to work on, and I felt so proud that I had come up with this one completely on my own.

The only person I had in mind when I wrote this was the memory of a nameless Morehouse student at a poetry slam asking women to smile more. It had only slightly annoyed me, but I decided to use that as my prompt to write him a response anyway. I hadn't intended to release it to the public immediately, only to see what my instructor thought of it.

After giving me nothing but praise and applause, she encouraged me to publish it in the CAU Review magazine and read it for the end-of-semester poetry slam she was organizing. It was both embarrassing and exciting, but I was glad to use it as a way of getting out of my comfort zone.

Fairy Tales

Here's a story about a boy
Who was destined to find love.
Far and wide, he looked for his chocolate bride.
He didn't mind if he'd be a little tall,
Nor a little wide.
He's found him.
Close to his dream, not all the way there.
He's made him a promise to be forever his
With a ring pop flavored with artificial berries
And feelings from the top of his pure heart.
Pure and sound.
And he crushed the ring pop into the ground
Until there were no longer little pieces of
strawberry-flavored candy,
But red dust that stained the ground.
Brokenhearted and down,
A guy he's not found has found him
At a place where people get drunk and have fun.

With him he's learned to dance.
With him he's learned to love.
But he was not the one,
For he wanted to adventure
And experience the world
In ways that didn't involve him,
But his friends in more ways than one.

Heart Notes

When did you realize someone wasn't the one? Some people realize too late, others think if they invest enough time and energy into a person, they'll eventually change into the person they've been wanting. The harsh reality is people change on their own time, not the time you grant them.

That's why it's so important to learn how to let the people you love go. When they come back to you, you'll both be completely different people with different mindsets than before. You let them go to allow for a chance to grow and develop themselves. This allows for the opportunity to come back as a better version than when they started.

If they don't come back, it's now your opportunity to grow for someone else.

4 + 9

I miss you every day that you're away from me,
but
I'm fighting my feelings
To stay away from you, but
Our chemistry is strong and I want to explore you.
I'm scared of you, but why?
Are you meant to tear down the walls that I'm
hiding behind?
What do we have in common
That isn't peace of mind?
What could you want from me
That another can't provide?
Your feelings were strong before, but
Did you put those feelings behind a door?
Would I ruin what we have over possibilities?
Have I let the words of others fall too far into me?
How would I feel if you
Betrothed yourself to another?

Could our situations switch?
Could I take you from her?
I'm selfish, I know,
But I don't think I'd be able to let you go.
Is you being here a sign? Another chance?
Am I messing up by making you my friend?
Have I brought someone in my life
Who is only in my way?
Please say ...
Say you still want me because I want you to stay
Am I crazy for thinking this way?
I spent two nights with you, but
Only one night was real.
I imagined the other.

Heart Notes

Was the grass ever greener on the other side? Sometimes when fear, desire, and uncertainty mix, we get a tangled mess of delusions imagining what could have been if decisions were different.

The haunting nature of unresolved connection, where chemistry lingers beneath the surface, but circumstances, or conscience, demand restraint. I wrestled with my own feelings of guilt, jealousy, and confusion, questioning whether I'm holding onto hope or dreams of how things work if I made different choices at certain times.

I wanted to be chosen, to be seen, but I needed to be sure I wasn't being selfish or destructive.

Ultimately, I wanted someone I wasn't supposed to have, and I imagined a reality that never came to be.

Lakee

You're beautiful.

You're passionate.

You're intelligent.

I miss you more than I'll ever

Be able to express to you.

And now that I've lost you,

I feel my heart squeeze itself in pain.

I love you, and I think I always will.

There is no getting over it,

No matter how many times I ignore you

Or you distance yourself from me.

I love you.

Heart Notes

If you could go back in time, what would you do differently? This poem is my quiet truth—a reflection of how love can remain even after someone is gone. I wrote it from a place of stillness, not to dramatize heartbreak, but to admit that I haven't stopped feeling.

This poem isn't about regret; it's about honoring what mattered. I learned that separation from someone doesn't have to mean your feelings change. Sometimes we separate ourselves from others to allow ourselves to learn from our experiences without hurting those around us.

About the Author

Beautiful V. Lawson is a proud New Orleans native and the 2017 National All-American Miss New Orleans City Queen. In 2023, she was recognized as a member of the National American Miss Maryland Queen's Court. A 2022 graduate of Clark Atlanta University, she earned her BFA in Theatre Arts and has since devoted her professional journey to service, education, and empowerment.

Beautiful is a former preschool educator turned federal government employee, currently pursuing her Master's Degree in Homeland Security. Her passion for uplifting others—especially young girls afraid to come out of their shells—has been a defining thread throughout her life. From mentoring incoming college students to leading community-based research initiatives, she has consistently used her voice and platform to advocate for resilience, self-expression, and social awareness.

Her work has been featured in *A New Renaissance: A Celebration of African American Fiction*. Beautiful continues to write from a place of deep introspection and cultural pride. Known for her unwavering discipline and organized approach, Beautiful believes in setting soft and hard deadlines to achieve her goals with excellence. She brings this same intentionality to her writing, using her experiences as a Black woman, scholar, and leader to inspire change and foster community.

Through pageantry, education, and public service as a proud member of Zeta Phi Beta Sorority, Incorporated, Beautiful Lawson stands as a testament to the power of perseverance and the beauty of purpose-driven living.